National Parks: **Brecon Beacons**

AF083653

Text: *Laura Hodgkinson*
Series editor: *Tony Bowerman*
Photographs: *Laura Hodgkinson, Shutterstock, Dreamstime, Alamy, Adobe Stock, Isla Hampson*

Design: *Carl Rogers and Laura Hodgkinson*

© Northern Eye Books Limited 2022

Laura Hodgkinson has asserted her rights under the Copyright, Designs and Patents Act, 1988 to be identified as the author of this work. All rights reserved.

This book contains mapping data licensed from the Ordnance Survey with the permission of the Controller of Her Majesty's Stationery Office. © Crown copyright 2022. All rights reserved. License number 100047867

Northern Eye Books

ISBN 978-1-914589-13-3

A CIP catalogue record for this book is available from the British Library.

www.northerneyebooks.co.uk

Cover: *Fan Brycheiniog & Picws Du (Walk 1)*

Important Advice: The routes described in this book are undertaken at the reader's own risk. Walkers should take into account their level of fitness, wear suitable footwear and clothing, and carry food and water. It is also advisable to take the relevant OS map with you in case you get lost and leave the area covered by our maps.

Whilst every care has been taken to ensure the accuracy of the route directions, the publishers cannot accept responsibility for errors or omissions, or for changes in the details given. Nor can the publisher and copyright owners accept responsibility for any consequences arising from the use of this book.

If you find any inaccuracies in either the text or maps, please write or email us at the address below. Thank you.

First published in 2022 by
Northern Eye Books Limited
Northern Eye Books, Tattenhall, Cheshire CH3 9PX

tony@northerneyebooks.co.uk

For sales enquiries, please call 01928 723 744

 @northerneyebooks
@lauraoutdoors

 @Northerneyeboo

Printed in the EU by Latitude on woodland-friendly FSC stock

Contents

The Brecon Beacons 4
Top 10 Walks: Brecon Beacons' best 6

1 | **Fan Brycheiniog & Picws Du** 8
2 | **Henrhyd Falls & Nant Llech** 14
3 | **The Four Waterfalls Walk** 20
4 | **Pen y Fan Horseshoe** 26
5 | **The Old Electric Shop** 32
6 | **Hay Bluff & Twmpa** 38
7 | **Blorenge** 42
8 | **Sugar Loaf** 46
9 | **Llanthony Priory** 52
10 | **The Skirrid Mountain Inn** 58

Useful Information 64

The Brecon Beacons

BRITAIN'S 10TH NATIONAL PARK was established in 1957 to preserve and highlight the unique landscape of the area. The Brecon Beacons National Park is supposedly named after the historical practice of lighting beacons of fire upon hilltops to forewarn neighbouring valleys of invasion.

The Brecon Beacons cover 1,344 square kilometres / 519 square miles with spectacular waterfalls, valleys and a huge expanse of hilly terrain: the Black Mountain to the west, Fforest Fawr Geopark, Waterfall Country and the Pen y Fan range at the centre, and the Black Mountains to the east.

The range of flora and fauna is as vast as the landscape. Rare arctic-alpine plants thrive within the unique upland environment. Unusual mammals found here include Welsh mountain ponies, greater and lesser horseshoe bats, otters and water voles. Birds of prey include the buzzard and red kite.

Cloud inversions from the Pen y Fan horseshoe

Brecon Beacons at their best

The ten walks in this book will take you to the most iconic and scenic areas of the Brecon Beacons National Park.

Experience everything this wild and spectacular part of South Wales has to offer, whether it's majestic summits and ancient forest, or thundering waterfalls and picturesque stream valleys.

But one thing's for sure: you're unlikely to forget a walk in the Brecon Beacons any time soon.

"Dod yn ôl at fy nghoed."

To become grounded, relaxed and calm.

Welsh Proverb

TOP 10 Walks: Brecon Beacons National Park

TEN OF THE VERY BEST WALKS IN THE BRECON BEACONS NATIONAL PARK are, quite literally, here within your grasp thanks to this pocket-sized book. Each circular walk has been carefully chosen to help you experience the very best this fantastic area of South Wales has to offer.

Whether you're looking for an exhilarating waterfall walk, a gentle hill walk, or something more challenging, you'll find it (and a lot more) right here.

RIDGE WALK — Fan Brycheiniog & Picws Du — page 8

WATERFALL WALK — Henrhyd Falls & Nant Llech — page 14

WATERFALL WALK — The Four Waterfalls Walk — page 20

MOUNTAIN WALK — Pen y Fan Horseshoe — page 26

TEA SHOP WALK — The Old Electric Shop — page 32	 **HILL WALK** — Hay Bluff & Twmpa — page 38
VIEWPOINT WALK — Blorenge — page 42 	**HILL WALK** — Sugar Loaf — page 46 
HISTORY WALK — Llanthony Priory & Hatterrall Ridge — page 52 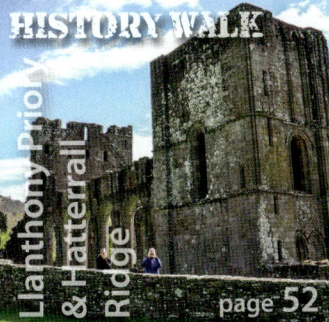	**PUB WALK** — The Skirrid Mountain Inn — page 58 

The towering ridgeline above Llyn y Fan Fach

RIDGE WALK

walk 1

Fan Brycheiniog & Picws Du

Fan Brycheiniog, Picws Du and the glacial lakes of Llyn y Fan Fach and Llyn y Fan Fawr

What to expect:
A good track leads to steep mountain paths. Navigation skills needed.

Distance/Time: 15 kilometres / 9 miles. Allow 5 hours

Start: Llyn y Fan Fach car park

Grid ref: SN 799 238

Ordnance Survey map: OS Explorer OL12 Brecon Beacons National Park *Western area*

After the walk: Red Lion Hotel, Felindre SA44 5UL | 01559 371677

Walk outline

A maintained track takes you uphill to the shores of Llyn y Fan Fach, where the route branches right up grassy hillside to gain the ridge of Bannau Sir Gaer and the Beacons Way footpath. Follow the crest of the ridge for some time and enjoy views of the north-facing cliffs below. Eventually reach the summit of Picws Du, before a steep descent and reascent takes you to Fan Brycheiniog, the highest point of this route. An eroded stone path curves downhill to join the pleasant water's edge of Llyn y Fan Fawr. The route follows the foot of the mountainside back to re-join the track.

Llyn y Fan Fawr

Glacial lakes

This walk visits two glacial lakes — Llyn y Fan Fach and Llyn y Fan Fawr. During the last Ice Age, over 11,000 years ago, this unique landscape of the Black Mountain was shaped by glaciers. The glacial snow and ice became trapped against the mountainside and loose rock, trapped within the ice, ground out the troughs. Later, the melting ice filled the troughs to form a series of glacial lakes.

Buzzard

The Walk

1. Take the obvious **gravel track** leading out of the car park. Continue uphill for roughly 1½ miles / 2.5 kilometres, following the riverside. Pass the **weir**, various water pools and small falls.

Ahead of you, the glacial trough and **prominent mountainside** of the route ahead comes into view.

2. Reach the shores of **Llyn y Fan Fach**.

Llyn y Fan Fach loosely translates to 'lake of the small mountain' — it is located at the base of Picws Du, the smaller summit on this route.

Just before the **stone rescue shelter**, take a right turn and follow the wide and well-worn path away from the lake and up **grassy hillside**.

Some walkers may take a tempting shortcut overland to meet this hillside path, but this doesn't save any time or effort due to the rough terrain, so is not recommended.

3. When the path levels out, bear left to join the **Beacons Way**. Continue walking along the crest of **Bannau Sir Gaer** with the **high cliffs** to your left and an expanse of open moorland to your right.

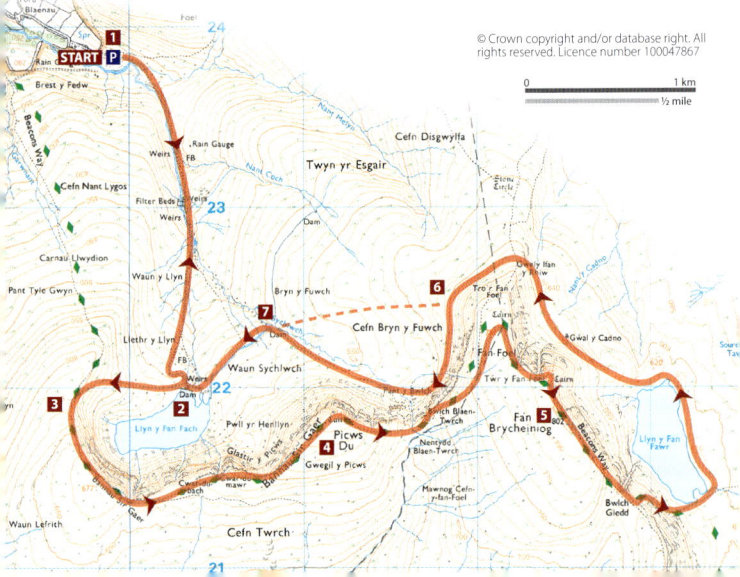

© Crown copyright and/or database right. All rights reserved. Licence number 100047867

Walk 1 – **Fan Brycheiniog** & **Picws Du** ♦ 11

Views from the grassy ridge of Bannau Sir Gaer

Don't worry if the idea of walking along the clifftop makes you nervous — you can keep as much distance as you need between yourself and the drop.

4. Arrive at the summit of **Picws Du** (749 metres / 2,457 feet), which juts out slightly from the main ridge and is marked with an ancient **stone cairn**.

Take a moment to absorb the spectacular views ahead towards Fan Brycheiniog and the rest of the Black Mountain range amongst the wider Brecon Beacons National Park.

Continue walking along the ridgeline. The path descends steeply **downhill** into the trough of **Bwlch Blaen-Twrch**.

Continue up the hillside ahead until you reach the subsidiary peak of **Fan-Foel**.

Follow the path south-east and arrive at the **trig point** marking the summit of **Fan Brycheiniog** (802.5 metres / 2,633 ft).

The terrain of this wild, mountainous area makes it a haven for birds. Skylarks are heard during warmer months while the red kite and common buzzard are present year-round. They are seen to fly on the rising thermal air around the cliff edges.

Ridgeline towards Picws Du

5. From the summit trig, continue south-east following the partly paved and graveled path.

When you reach the end of the **fence**, follow the descent path that curves round to the left.

There is a red kite feeding station nearby at Llanddeusant. Keep your eyes on the sky to increase your chances of spotting one or visit the feeding station. Red kites have become an icon of south and mid Wales.

Reach the idyllic shores of **Llyn y Fan Fawr** and follow the path around to the far side of the lake. The route branches off **slightly uphill** in a north-westerly direction from the lakeside.

The path may become unclear, especially in foggy conditions. Don't stray too far from the foot of Fan Foel and you'll have little issue.

Continue along the path as it curves below the foot of the mountains you've just travelled over.

Llyn y Fan Fawr loosely translates to 'lake of the large mountain' – it sits below Fan Brycheiniog, the highest point in the Black Mountain (802 metres / 2,631 feet).

6. At the **junction** in the path, swing **left** and walk below the cliffs of Picws Du.

Alternatively, you could go straight ahead at the junction to take the shortcut highlighted with a dotted line. It is a popular path for those looking for a quicker route between Llyn y Fan Fawr and Llyn y Fan Fach.

Reach the **small dam** and waterway.

7. Follow the **waterway** in a south-westerly direction leading you back to Llyn y Fan Fach.

Rejoin the **gravel track** to return to your starting point. ♦

The Lady of the Lake
According to Welsh legend, a young man grazing cattle at Llyn y Fan Fach witnessed a beautiful woman rise from the lake. He asked her to be his wife and she agreed on one condition: that he would not hit her more than three times. Of course, the husband accidentally inflicted three blows and so his wife and her animals returned to the lake. The indents from an animal-led plough can still be seen.

Walking behind Henrhyd Falls

WATERFALL WALK

walk 2

Henrhyd Falls & Nant Llech

A pleasant wander through Graig Llech forest leading you to Henrhyd Falls, the highest waterfall in South Wales

What to expect:
Quiet lanes, forest path with wooden walkways and steps

Distance/time: 5.6 kilometres / 3½ miles. Allow 2–3 hours

Start: Henrhyd Falls National Trust car park

Grid ref: SN 853 121

Ordnance Survey Map: OS Explorer OL12 Brecon Beacons National Park *Western area*

After the walk: Gwyn Arms, Glyntawe, Penycae SA9 1GP | 01639 730310

Walk outline

Begin with a quiet walk along country lanes towards Ynyswen and take a short detour to enjoy views of the River Tawe. Return to the lane and enter the peaceful Graig Llech forest, an SSSI (Site of Special Scientific Interest) thanks to the variety of ferns, mosses and fossils found along the riverbed. The route leads up the wooded valley before arriving at Henrhyd Falls. Walking this route anti-clockwise and leaving the waterfall to the end avoids an uphill slog at the end of the walk.

Henrhyd Falls

Henrhyd Falls, or Sgwd Henrhyd in Welsh, is the highest waterfall in South Wales with a drop of 90 feet / 27 metres. It is possible to walk behind the falls if water levels allow — during times of heavy rain the path can be out of bounds but this is made up for by the sight of the falls in full flow! Either way, the falls offer a unique experience and photography opportunities of one of the most impressive waterfalls in the Brecon Beacons National Park.

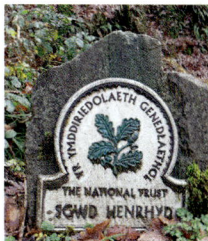

Sgwd Henrhyd

Behind the falls

The Walk

1. Leave the National Trust car park onto the quiet road and turn left.

Take the next left down the single-track **country lane**. Fine views open up across the Cribarth hillside above the village of Ynyswen.

Sheep are common across Wales and are farmed for their milk, fleece and meat. Flocks of sheep are still rounded up the traditional way with trained sheepdogs. At the time of writing, the world record for the most expensive sheepdog is held by a Welsh border collie sold for an eye-watering £27,000.

2. Arrive at the **kissing gate** on your right signed for 'Abercraf Ynyswen'.

To take the detour to the **River Tawe**, follow the path through the kissing gate until you come to the bridge over the river — a lovely spot for a break.

The River Tawe (Afon Tawe in Welsh) flows downstream through Swansea before emerging into the Bristol Channel. The river is 30 miles / 48 kilometres in length.

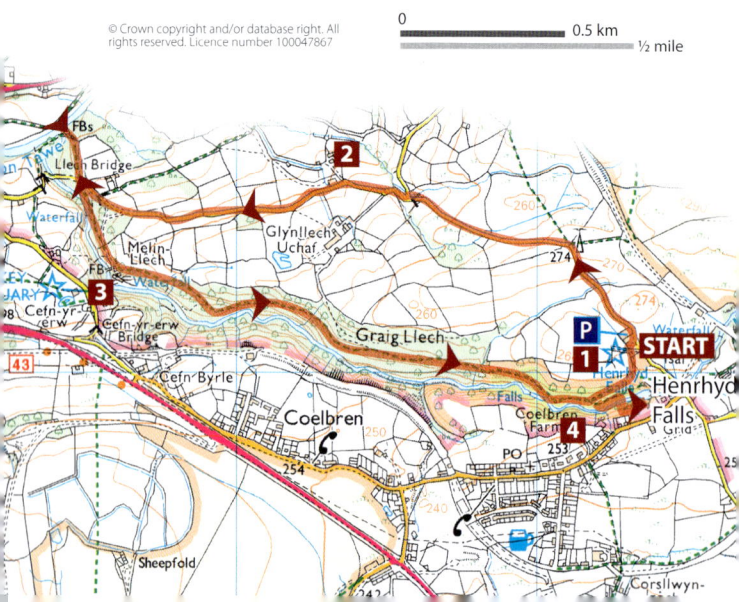

Walk 2 – **Henrhyd Falls** & **Nant Llech** ♦ 17

Taking a break at Henrhyd Falls

When you are ready, retrace your steps back to the road.

3. Take the opposite footpath signed for 'Waterfall' that leads you through the **kissing gate** and into the **Craig Llech forest**.

In spring and summer, you won't need reminding to look around at the variety of forest and riverside-dwelling birds. Spot wagtails, warblers, dippers and even woodpeckers. Travel quietly to increase your chances of seeing them.

Walk onwards and ascend the stepped pathway to arrive at Melin Llech. Note the **small waterfall** and bridge.

Melin Llech (slate mill) is a disused water mill. Wool from local farms was once processed and spun into cloth here by harnessing the power of the river. watermills were once common in South Wales and provided an essential aid to developing local industry.

Do not take the bridge, but continue on the path leading you beneath the ruins of Melin Llech and then along the banks of **Nant Llech**.

Henrhyd Falls

Nant Llech loosely translates to 'slab stream'; likely a direct reference to the flat sandstone slabs beneath its flow. Sandstone is a soft rock which is easily eroded by moving water.

4. Continue making your way steadily uphill through the wooded valley. The forest is mostly made up of old oak and ash trees.

Pass through various gates, walkways and footbridges until you arrive at the **sign posted junction**.

Continue ahead / slight right here along the valley floor. It is signed for 'Waterfall'.

Ancient fossilised trees were found during an 1800s' geological survey in the Nant Llech valley (Cwm Llech). They are now kept on display in the Swansea Museum gardens (www.swanseamuseum.co.uk).

Cross the **wooden bridge** and continue up the steep, stepped walkway.

Arrive at the foot of the magnificent **Henrhyd Falls**.

Film buffs will recognise Henrhyd Falls as the 'Bat Cave' in the 2012 Batman film 'The Dark Knight Rises'. Although it is possible to walk behind the falls, as Bruce Wayne does in the film, there is unfortunately no secret cave there.

To walk behind the falls, you must follow the rough path to the right, though this is not advisable when the falls are in heavy flow or if there is a chance of loose ground.

5. Retrace your steps back over the bridge and swing right up the wide, steep path.

Follow the path through the **gate** to return to your starting point. ♦

A Taste of Wales
Penderyn single-malt Welsh whisky has been distilled in South Wales since the year 2000. Over the years, Penderyn whisky has become one of Wales's best-loved exports and is enjoyed by whisky connoisseurs and curious tasters all over the world. You can try it for yourself at the Penderyn Whisky Visitor Centre and Distillery Shop located in the nearby village of Penderyn (CF44 0SX, www.penderyn.wales).

Sgwd yr Eira

WATERFALL WALK

walk 3

The Four Waterfalls Walk

An easy-to-follow waterfall trail taking you to Sgwd Clun-Gwyn, Sgwd y Pannwr, Sgwd Isaf Clun-Gwyn and Sgwd yr Eira

What to expect:
Waymarked forest tracks and paths; mixed terrain underfoot, care required at the riverside

Distance/time: 9 kilometres / 5½ miles. Allow 3–4 hours

Start: Gwaun Hepste pay and display car park

Grid ref: SN 935 123

Ordnance Survey Map: OS Explorer OL12 Brecon Beacons National Park *Western area*

After the walk: The New Inn, Ystradfellte CF44 9JE | 01639 721014

Walk outline:
A half-day walk along the banks of the River Hepste where you will discover four spectacular waterfalls. Begin on a wide, well-maintained forest track before descending downhill to join the main gorge-side path. Each waterfall is reached by a linear trail off this main path, resulting in several short and steep sections throughout this walk. Perhaps the most exhilarating part of the route is the opportunity to walk behind the curtain-like falls of Sgwd yr Eira. Return to the car park along wide forest tracks.

Orientation panel

Waterfall Country
Experience a true piece of the ancient Welsh landscape; thundering waterfalls hidden from civilisation by deep forest-lined gorges and valleys dotted with clues of a rich industrial past. Waterfall Country encapsulates an area in the south-west of the National Park where waterfalls and rivers are most common. Many walkers choose the Four Waterfalls Walk as their first experience of Waterfall Country, and for good reason — you can almost always hear the falls before you see them. Plus, there is the lure of seeing four waterfalls in this one walk.

Dipper

The Walk

1. Begin this classic trail by taking the **wide track** next to the information boards.

Continue ahead on the forest track, ignoring any footpaths that you cross, following the red and green 'Four Falls Trail' **waymarkers**.

Bear right at the signpost signed 'Sgwd Clun-Gwyn 17 mins' and descend steeply downhill amongst tall **evergreen forest**.

Reach another signpost, and continue straight ahead, signed for **Sgwd Clun-Gwyn**.

Throughout this walk you will come across information boards offering helpful descriptions of the path ahead as well as timescales to the next waterfall on the route, making this a good family walk for those who may take a little longer than anticipated to complete the trail.

2. Descend straight ahead at another **signpost**, following the sound of the roaring water.

Arrive at the viewpoint overlooking **Sgwd Clun-Gwyn** (fall of the white meadow), the first waterfall you will visit on this trail.

© Crown copyright and/or database right. All rights reserved. Licence number 100047867

Walk 3 – **The Four Waterfalls Walk**

Sgwd y Pannwr

View the turbulent waters from above before retracing your steps back to the last signpost. Turn right for 'Sgwd yr Eira 30 mins'. Cross the small and **shallow stream** with some stepping-stones.

The route is waymarked again with red and green arrows, leading through ancient oak woodland and then over a **wooden walkway**.

Continue on as the path leads you along the upper banks of the gorge and past **Coedydd Nedd**, an ancient and diverse sessile oak forest.

3. At the **information board** take the downhill path to the right, waymarked with green arrows and signed for 'Sgwd y Pannwr 15 mins'.

After around 0.5 kilometres / 500 metres of downhill you now arrive at **Sgwd y Pannwr**.

The flat, naturally eroded rock surface here is unique to this waterfall on the trail. Explore the rocky and exposed riverside before gazing across at the expansive waterfall from this vantage point.

Sgwd Isaf Clun-Gwyn

Follow the path upstream, hugging the riverside, and arrive at the magnificent **Sgwd Isaf Clun-Gwyn**.

Don't be tempted to take a shortcut up the hillside here; the scrambling can be tricky and it does not save time due to the difficult terrain.

Retrace your steps past Sgwd y Pannwr and back up to the main path.

At the signpost turn right for Sgwd yr Eira, the last waterfall of the walk.

4. Bear right at the path junction. It is signed for 'Sgwd yr Eira 8 mins'.

Descend the steep, stepped path until you reach **Sgwd yr Eira** — possibly the most impressive waterfall on this route and certainly well worth the effort.

If you're feeling adventurous and water levels are not too high, walk towards the left side of the falls to join a rocky path leading behind the waterfall.

Sgwd yr Eira translates to 'falls of snow', likely due to how the water appears when you are stood behind it looking out; a surreal sight that not many people are lucky enough to experience. It also offers some unique photo opportunities from both sides of the falls and photographers often visit here for this reason alone.

Retrace your steps back to the main path and then turn slight right, signed for 'Gwaun Hepste car park 55 mins', again following the red and green **waymarkers**. The path leads you away from the gorge and uphill into the forest.

Continue following signposts for **Gwaun Hepste** to be led back to your starting point. ♦

Mighty Oaks

Oak trees have always been an integral part of Welsh and British history and have, over the years, become a symbol of endurance, royalty, wisdom and strength — the oldest oak trees can live for up to 1,000 years. Interestingly, acorns were once used to grind into flour and were even dried to make a powdered hot drink — perhaps an ancient version of hot chocolate!

Golden hour on the Pen y Fan horseshoe

MOUNTAIN WALK

Pen y Fan Horseshoe

walk 4

A challenging circular ridge walk across Fan y Big, Cribyn, Pen y Fan and Corn Du

What to expect:
A bridleway, some good paths. Navigation skills essential

Distance/Time: 16 kilometres / 10 miles. Allow 6 hours

Start: Forestry Commission car park at Taf Fechan Forest

Grid ref: SO 038 169

Ordnance Survey map: OS Explorer OL12 Brecon Beacons National Park *Western area*

After the walk: The Old Barn Tearoom, Ystradgynwyn, Torpantau CF48 2UT | 01685 373175

Walk outline

There are few, if any, mountain walks this spectacular in the Brecon Beacons. Begin on a bridleway, slowly gaining height before branching off to the summit of Fan y Big and its famous 'diving board'. A sharp descent and immediate ascent takes you to Cribyn before one last push to gain the summits of Pen y Fan and neighbouring Corn Du. A gentle sloping ridge takes you back down the other side of the glacial valley. This is probably the most challenging walk in this book.

Pen y Fan

Pen y Fan loosely translates to 'the top peak' or 'head of the peak' in Welsh and is the highest mountain in South Wales at a lofty 886 metres / 2,906 feet. Locals as well as visitors from all across the UK and beyond frequent the mountain year-round. Walkers are spoilt for choice when choosing a route to walk up Pen y Fan, with the busiest option being the linear route from Pont ar Daf car park which has become affectionately known as 'The Motorway'. The walk in this book takes a quieter and arguably more scenic route to Pen y Fan.

Pen y Fan summit

Pen y Fan horseshoe

The Walk

© Crown copyright and/or database right. All rights reserved. Licence number 10004786

1. Exit the car park at the far end, next to a **boulder**, and bear left along the road.

Shortly, turn right up the **bridleway** following the edge of the forest.

This section is believed to be an old Roman Road leading directly through the Welsh mountains.

Come to the gate and climb over the **stile**. Cross the small river and continue on ahead.

Views towards Pen y Fan and the rest of the horseshoe are visible towards the head of this scenic valley. Spot Upper Neuadd Reservoir below, currently drained of water. This is to help protect its Grade II listed building.

2. Arrive at the saddle of **Bwlch ar y Fan** (which loosely translates to 'pass of the hill or beacon') and take the obvious path to the right leading you steeply uphill to the summit of **Fan y Big** ('point of the hill or beacon').

Those brave enough may choose to step onto the 'Diving Board' for a memorable photo opportunity — it's a

Walk 4 – **Pen y Fan Horseshoe** ♦ 29

The 'Diving Board' on Fan y Big

great, flat slab of rock with epic views of Cribyn and the face of Pen y Fan in the background.

Spend some time enjoying the fantastic views before retracing your steps back down to Bwlch ar y Fan.

Continue directly ahead up the steep and eroded path and along the crest of **Craig Cwm Cynwyn** ridge to gain the summit of **Cribyn**.

Here is the best vantage point to take in the impressive north-east face of Pen y Fan which you will shortly be stood a-top of.

Drag your gaze skyward and you may spot a magnificent red kite. Listen out for the unique 'mewing' noise made by these once rare birds of prey. They can be recognised fairly easily from a distance by their large forked tail.

Leave Cribyn summit by taking the obvious path south-west.

The steep downhill eventually levels out at the saddle of **Craig Cwm Sere**.

Continue up the steep well-maintained path ahead, gaining the summit ridge to **Pen y Fan** and it's large Bronze Age **burial cairn**.

Pen y Fan from above

Burial cairns — or burial mounds — are a regular sight on the mountain tops of South Wales. These Welsh burial cairns can be dated back to anywhere between 2,300 – 800BC.

3. Take the wide path south-west from the summit and descend towards Corn Du — the second highest summit in the Brecon Beacons standing at 873 metres.

This section of the route forms part of the **Beacons Way** — a long-distance trekking route across the Brecon Beacons National Park that you may be tempted to return to tackle someday.

On a clear day you will be able to enjoy panoramic views of the Black Mountain to the west, the Elan Valley to the north-west, the Bristol Channel to the south, and of course the rest of the Brecon Beacons.

Branch right at the fork in the trail and make your way up the hand-railed path to reach the flat summit of **Corn Du**.

Descend in a southerly direction, following the path.

Cross the main tourist path and continue towards the often-overlooked **Bwlch Duwynt**.

Walk down the grassy ridges of **Craig Gwaun Taf** and **Graig Fan Ddu**.

4. Eventually, reach the head of the **forest tree line** and turn left down the steep path.

Walk 4 – **Pen y Fan Horseshoe**

Continue down the now excellent path and through the **gate**.

Make your way through the series of old **pump house** buildings at the foot of the reservoir.

Turn right onto the **private road**.

Continue along the road to return back to your starting point. ♦

The Welsh Three Peaks
The Welsh Three Peaks challenge involves climbing the three highest peaks in Wales. The challenge takes in the mountains of Snowdon (the highest mountain in Wales and England), Cadair Idris in southern Snowdonia, and Pen y Fan in the Brecon Beacons. Many attempt to climb all three within 24 hours (with a driver to take them between each location) but others may take longer.

The Old Electric Shop and Café

TEA SHOP WALK

The Old Electric Shop

walk 5

What to expect:
Easy-going paths and walkways, some surfaced pavements

Wander along the banks of the River Wye in Hay-on-Wye and enjoy a refreshment at The Old Electric Shop and Café

Distance/time: 2.4 kilometres / 1½ miles. Allow 1–2 hours
Start: Oxford Road car park (pay & display)
Grid ref: SO 229 422
Ordnance Survey Map: OS Explorer OL13 Brecon Beacons National Park *Eastern area*
The Café: The Old Electric Shop and Café, Hay-on-Wye, HR3 5DB | 01497 821194 | www.oldelectric.co.uk

Walk outline
Make your way along quiet pavements and winding footpaths, passing St Mary's Church, to the banks of the River Wye. Continue following a clear public footpath and cross a field to walk across The Warren — a site of Special Scientific Interest due to its abundance of wildlife including kingfishers and even otters. Pass pebbled beaches and shaded trees as you meander along the riverside, following the River Wye back towards the town. The route then takes you through the historical town centre of Hay-on-Wye, with the opportunity for a refreshment at The Old Electric Shop and Café before returning past Hay Castle.

Coffee and cakes

▶ The Old Electric Shop and Café at a glance
Open: Every day 10am–5pm
Food and Specialties: Locally sourced modern vegetarian food, freshly baked bread and cakes. Vegan and gluten free options
Beverages: Locally roasted coffee, Fair-Trade loose-leaf tea, herbal teas, soft drinks
Children and dogs: Well behaved children and dogs welcome. 'Babychino's' are available

Tasty lunches

The Walk

1. Take the footpath from the bottom corner of the car park, below the **primary school**.

Bear right at the road. At the next road, bear right again.

Look out for the **wooden footpath sign** on the wall of the **stone building** shortly on your left.

Take this footpath leading over a series of small bridges and wells before emerging outside **St Mary's Church**.

Continue through the **gate** at the right of the 15th century church's entrance and walk along the shaded footpath. The old church wall and grounds are on your left.

Go underneath the **old railway** — through what looks like a small tunnel — and then bear left at the footpath signed for 'Y Warren / The Warren'.

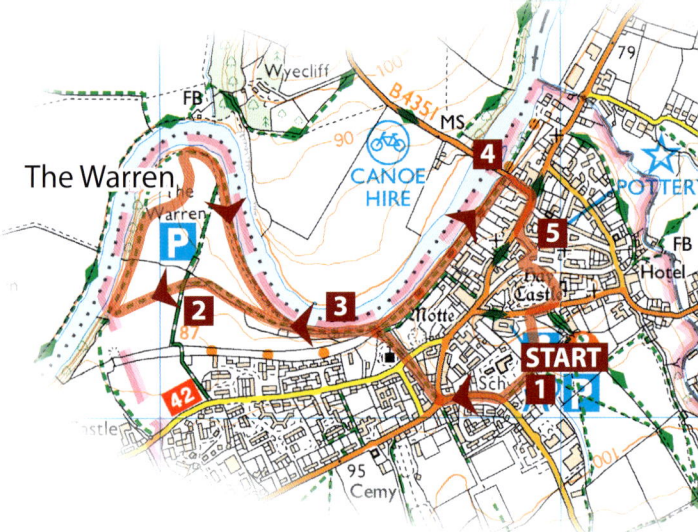

Walk 5 – **The Old Electric Shop & Café, Hay-on-Wye** ♦ 35

Hay on Wye is rightly known as 'the town of books'

Pass by the quaint **cottage** on your left and then go through the gate.

Keep left at the split in the path and continue ahead.

2. Cross the bridleway and carry on through the **gate** straight ahead, following the path through the field.

Go through another gate and turn right along the upper banks of the **River Wye**.

Walk between some **benches** before bearing left to reach the riverside.

The path curves around to the right alongside the river. Walk past several **pebble 'beaches'** at the water's edge.

Ignore any paths to the right and stay on the gentle footpath at the riverside.

3. Go through the gate and walk past the **cottage** passed earlier in the walk. Continue ahead at the signpost for 'River walk'.

Stay on the wide footpath, passing **wooden sculptures** of local wildlife hidden amongst the trees, ignoring any rough paths that may branch off.

Summer on the tranquil River Wye

These wooden sculptures are all thanks to the Hay Community Woodland Group and were carved into shape by Welsh chainsaw sculptors. Some of the expertly carved animals you may spot include an otter, multiple owls, and a heron.

4. Arrive below the B4351 **road bridge** with **The Bean Box** to the right.

Take the footpath signed for 'Toilets' leading slightly uphill under the bridge.

At the road, bear left and walk along the pavement.

At the next road junction, turn right towards the town centre.

The **Old Electric Shop and Café** is shortly on your right.

Hay-on-Wye is often referred to as a 'booktown'. It hosts The Hay Festival of Literature & Arts, better known as Hay Festival, every year. The town is home to numerous book shops.

5. From The Old Electric Shop's doorway, cross the road and turn right. Walk a short distance along the pavement.

Bear a slight left at the **Hay Town Clock** and walk up the pedestrianised area next to **The Poetry Book Shop**, signed for 'Car Park'.

Take the next right and walk a short distance until you reach Shepherds Ice Cream Parlour and **Hay Castle** opposite.

To return to the car park, follow the large **'Car Park' sign** to the left of the castle.

Keep bearing right until you spot the car park entrance on the left. Return to your starting point. ♦

Hay Castle
Hay Castle (Castell y Gelli) can be dated back to the time of The Normans invasion in the late 11th century. More recent years saw the addition of a large Jacobean manor house to the original castle. Today the castle, manor and its grounds are owned by the Hay Castle Trust who aim to preserve and care for the site as a cultural and historical landmark.

Views from Twmpa

HILL WALK

walk 6

Hay Bluff & Twmpa

A pleasant half-day hill walk to visit two popular summits; a perfect introduction to walking in the Black Mountains

What to expect:
Mostly good paths with excellent views. Some navigation needed

Distance/time: 9.5 kilometres / 6 miles. Allow 3½ - 4½ hours

Start: Hay Bluff parking area at a stone circle, above Hay-on-Wye

Grid ref: SO 239 373

Ordnance Survey Map: OS Explorer OL13 Brecon Beacons National Park *Eastern area*

After the walk: The Old Black Lion, Hay-on-Wye HR3 5AD | 01497 82084

Walk outline
Park at the stone circle and take the obvious path up Hay Bluff opposite, which zig-zags steeply uphill to reach the summit 'trig' point. Walk along the edge of the mountainside via an excellent path offering wonderful views across the countryside. The path descends to cross the road at Gospel Pass, and continues steadily uphill to reach the summit of Twmpa (also known as Lord Hereford's Knob). A grassy descent path leads down and around the mountainside, through open pastureland, and then a short distance along a quiet road.

Hay Bluff
At the very eastern edge of the Brecon Beacons lie the Black Mountains, a wild and high expanse of open hill, steep inclines and panoramic views. Home to hardy mountain ponies and sheep, Hay Bluff reaches a summit height of 677 metres / 2,221 feet. Its impressive stature allows for excellent views across the Wye Valley, the Black Mountain range in the west, and, on a clear day, mid-Wales and beyond.

Hay Bluff 'trig' point

Mountain ponies

The Walk

1. From the stone circle parking area, cross the road and take the steep, **obvious path** up the mountainside.

The path curves to the right and improves into a good quality gravel path underfoot.

At the path junction, swing left to gain the high path leading to the top of **Hay Bluff**. The top is easily recognised by a **white cairn sporting a red dragon**.

2. From Hay Bluff summit, retrace your steps a short distance and then continue ahead along the good path following the edge of the mountainside — named **Ffynnon y Parc** on the OS map.

Views ahead encompass the mountains beyond and the south-east of the Brecon Beacons National Park. Twmpa is the next hill in view and your next destination on this circular walk.

3. After just under a mile / about 1.5 kilometres of easy walking, descend towards **Gospel Pass**.

Cross the road and continue up the opposite hillside to join the good path.

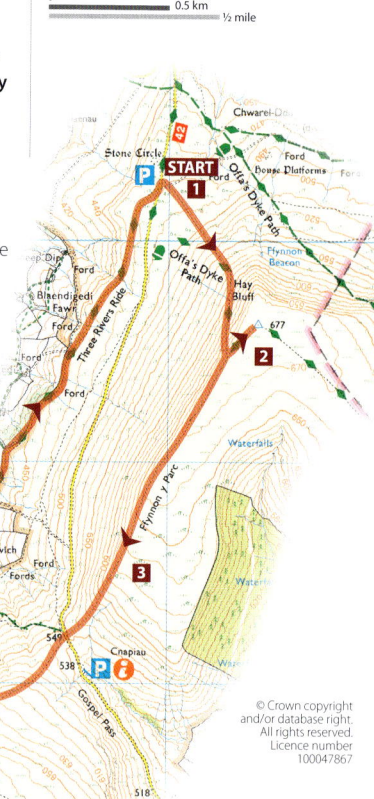

© Crown copyright and/or database right. All rights reserved. Licence number 100047867

Taking a break before the descent to Gospel Pass

Continue to climb steadily uphill towards the grassy hilltop **Twmpa** which is distinguished by a small cairn.

Begin your descent by taking the south-west path from Twmpa's summit.

4. The path now levels out. Take the right turning here which traverses downhill to the grassland below.

When the ground begins to level out, take the **rough path** to the right which skirts below Twmpa before briefly meeting a broader path.

5. Walk left now for a short distance and you will meet the **quiet lane**.

Turn right and follow the lane back to your starting point. ♦

Red kites

Red kites are a medium-sized bird of prey that can be easily recognised by their angular tail and wings, red and brown markings, and their 'mewing' call. They prey on small mammals, such as mice, voles and rabbits. Red kites were once hunted near to extinction but there are now over 300 breeding pairs in Wales thanks to years of conservation efforts.

Panoramic views from Blorenge

VIEWPOINT WALK

walk 7

Blorenge

What to expect:
Mixed paths, quiet roads

An easy-going option to climb Blorenge from Keepers Pond to enjoy this popular viewpoint

Distance/time: 5 kilometres / 3 miles. Allow 2 hours

Start: Keepers Pond car park

Grid ref: SO 254 107

Ordnance Survey Map: OS Explorer OL13 Brecon Beacons National Park *Eastern area*

After the walk: The Bridge Inn, Llanfoist NP7 9LH | 01873 854831 | www.bridgellanfoist.com

Walk outline

From Keepers Pond car park, make your way along a quiet road and up a good path with gentle terrain. An ancient burial chamber marks the highest point of this walk at Blorenge summit. Descend down the hillside to the road, before a gentle walk back to the car park. This memorable outing will treat you to wonderful views in all directions. Consider enjoying this circular route on a summer evening when the trails are quieter and the evening birdsong can add to an already lovely walk.

Blorenge

This delightful hill walk is popular with locals and visitors alike due to its straightforward access, fantastic views and the variety of interesting sights, flora and fauna to discover along the route. Blorenge, also known as The Blorenge, stands at an elevation of 1,841 foot / 561 metres above sea level, although the car parks are located a good way up the mountainside saving you much of the uphill effort if walked from the very bottom. You'll be able to see the hills of Sugarloaf and The Skirrid from the summit plateau; two of the other hill walks offered in this book.

Paraglider

Welsh mountain sheep

The Walk

1. Leave the **Keepers Pond** car park and walk left along the road. Take another left after roughly 150 metres.

Look out for the **radio masts** on your right opposite **Foxhunter car park**.

Take the obvious path from the far end of Foxhunter car park. In busy times you could also park here to begin the walk.

Foxhunter was a show jumping horse, ridden by Welshman Harry Llewellyn. He was known for winning Britain's only gold medal at the 1952 Olympics. Foxhunter's memorial is located just a short distance from the car park.

2. Gain height steadily as you continue along the easy-to-follow path.

The route underfoot eventually becomes more eroded, a sign that you are approaching the highest point of the walk.

A **white trig point** and a Bronze Age burial chamber mark your arrival at Blorenge summit. Take a break at this viewpoint and enjoy the panoramic views in every direction.

3. From the white trig point at Blorenge summit, take the **faint path** heading north-east.

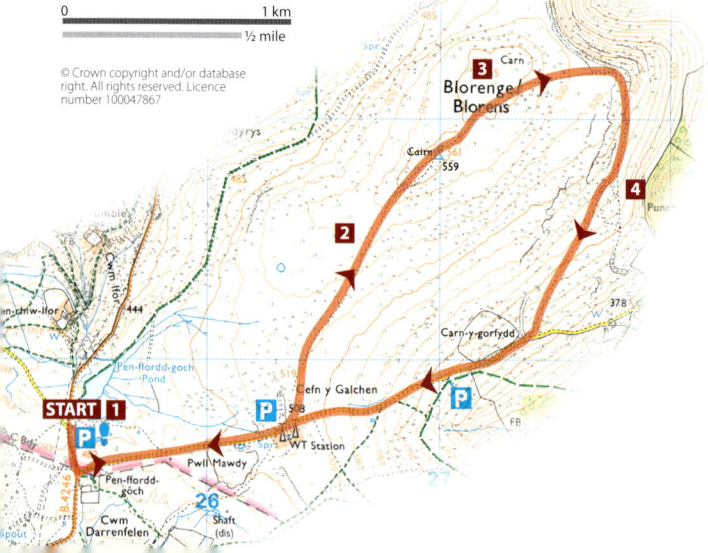

Keepers Pond

The path widens and improves as you descend the hillside.

Continue downhill and past the small **Mountain Rescue building** on the left.

Follow the path as it curves slightly to the right to join the **deep-set track**.

On a clear day you can take in views over the Punchbowl pond, a sheltered haven for wildlife and birdlife, and the Usk Valley further below.

4. At the obvious fork in the route, take the right-hand **track** downhill to reach the road.

Bear right at the road and walk back to Keepers Pond and your starting point. ♦

Wild ponies

Welsh mountain ponies were originally employed as 'pit ponies' in coal mines and as working ponies on farms across Wales. In recent decades, the ponies are in less demand for these roles and so many live their lives roaming free in the Welsh landscape. Farmers help with the management and care of these semi-wild mountain ponies to ensure their continued survival.

Sugar Loaf summit ridge

HILL WALK

walk 8

Sugar Loaf

This circular walk takes you on one of the more scenic routes to the popular summit of Sugar Loaf

What to expect:
Good paths and tracks through open access land, expansive views

Distance/time: 8 kilometres/ 5 miles. Allow 3 hours

Start: National Trust car park at Mynydd Llanwenarth

Grid ref: SO 268 167

Ordnance Survey Map: OS Explorer OL13 Brecon Beacons National Park *Eastern area*

After the walk: Sugar Loaf Vineyards & Café, NP77LA | 01873 853066

Walk outline

Ascend a gently sloping track which, after a mile or so, drops down and across a stream. Join a path curving north-east towards Mynydd Pen-y-fâl (the original Welsh name for Sugar Loaf). This section is much quieter than taking the main route directly to the summit. The good path leads through unique blocks of rock before arriving at the white summit cairn of Sugar Loaf. A steep descent with a birds-eye view of Abergavenny gives way to gentle slopes leading walkers back to the car park at Mynydd Llanwenarth.

Sugar Loaf

It's position amongst the highest points in the Black Mountains makes Sugar Loaf (569 m / 1955 ft) more than worth the effort to climb and it is therefore a deservedly popular hill. It is located on the southern fringe of the Black Mountains and walkers can enjoy views over nearby hills, such as The Skirrid to the east, and the Bristol Channel to the south. Panoramic views in every direction are only obscured by the occasional bird soaring by at eye-level.

Descending Sugar Loaf

Wheatear

48 ♦ TOP 10 WALKS **NATIONAL PARKS: Brecon Beacons**

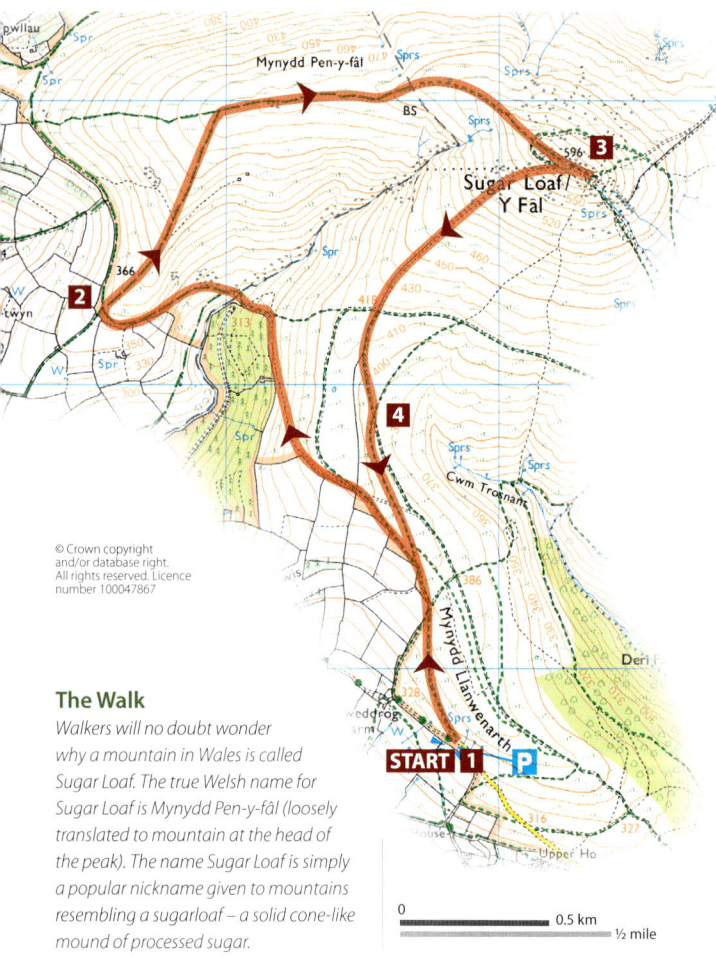

© Crown copyright and/or database right. All rights reserved. Licence number 100047867

The Walk

Walkers will no doubt wonder why a mountain in Wales is called Sugar Loaf. The true Welsh name for Sugar Loaf is Mynydd Pen-y-fâl (loosely translated to mountain at the head of the peak). The name Sugar Loaf is simply a popular nickname given to mountains resembling a sugarloaf – a solid cone-like mound of processed sugar.

Walk 8 – **Sugar Loaf** ♦ 49

Rock formations on Sugar Loaf

1. From the parking area at Mynydd Llanwenarth, take the clear, wide track to the left of the **information board**.

Stay on the track loosely following an **old stone wall**.

Ignore the numerous grassy trails that lead off to the right; one of these will be your return route.

The imposing summit of Sugar Loaf has come into view. It is 596 metres / 1,955 ft in height. That's just 4 metres too short to be considered a true mountain.

The rocky track eventually narrows and curves left.

After a short, steep downhill section the route crosses over a **stream**.

Ascend uphill again for a short distance. You are still to the right of the old **stone wall**.

There is a small vineyard at the base of Sugar Loaf. They produce a range of local wines and have an on-site café. Visit for a stroll around the vineyard, a light lunch, or a taste of their award-winning wines (www.sugarloafvineyards.co.uk).

Sugar Loaf birds-eye view

2. At the path **junction** next to the gate in the wall, bear an immediate right up the **grassy hillside**.

Walk steadily through low-lying bilberry bushes dotted with their edible dark-blue berries during late summer and into early autumn.

Gain the grassy, sloping ridge of **Pen-y-Fâl** and bear right onto the path towards Sugar Loaf summit.

3. Pass through **blocky rocks** as you arrive at the top of **Sugar Loaf**, marked by a **white trig point**.

The majority of Sugar Loaf consists of red sandstone, which is soft and easily eroded. However, the very top consists of more robust quartz conglomerate which has resisted erosion. This is the reason why Sugar Loaf has remained one of the higher hills in this area.

Walk a few metres south-east of the summit and bear a tight right to join the eroded descent **path**.

The path will widen, the ground will level out and underfoot will become grassy again.

Continue walking ahead through the footpath **junction**.

4. At the second **smaller footpath junction**, bear right along the faint path to meet the track you started the walk on.

Bear left along the track, with the old stone wall on your right, to return to your starting point. ♦

House martins

House martins can be spotted in the skies around Sugar Loaf and its neighbouring villages and towns between April and October. Look out for their white chin and lower back, dark wings, and a shorter, wider tail than a swallow. As their name suggests, house martins often nest in the eaves of houses where they build their nests from mud, twigs, sheep's wool and grass.

The 13th century ruins of Llanthony Priory

HISTORY WALK

walk 9

Llanthony Priory

Admire the priory before walking along Hatterrall Ridge. Finish the walk with a real ale at Llanthony Priory's cellar bar

What to expect:
Some signposts, good paths, steep descent

Distance/time: 9.5 kilometres/ 6 miles. Allow 3.5-4 hours

Start: Free car park at Llanthony Priory

Grid ref: SO 289 278

Ordnance Survey Map: OS Explorer OL13 Brecon Beacons National Park *Eastern area*

After the walk: Llanthony Priory Hotel restaurant & cellar bar. Closed Mondays. 01873 890487 | www.llanthonyprioryhotel.co.uk

Walk outline

Take signposted paths through open fields before curving up and around the ruins of Siarpal — believed to be an uncompleted mansion house from the 1800's. Briefly join the Beacons Way gaining height quickly towards Hatterrall Ridge. Take the Offa's Dyke path north offering fine views of the surrounding hills and valleys in all directions. Eventually, descend a grassy ridge above Loxidge Wood that leads back down towards Llanthony Priory. Your reward awaits at the priory's cellar bar set amongst the 13th century priory ruins.

Llanthony Priory

900-year-old Llanthony Priory is hidden deep within the wooded Vale of Ewyas amongst the Black Mountains. The site has lost little of its prominence over the years despite the comparatively modern additions of a hotel, farm and chapel (the Church of St. David's); it is clear to see how impressive the priory and its grounds would once have been when admiring its lofty arches and highly skilled stonework. The priory ruins themselves are now cared for and maintained by Cadw.

Llanthony signpost

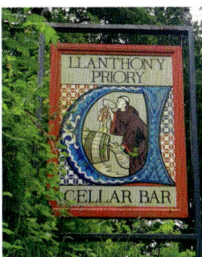

Llanthony cellar bar

The Walk

1. Walk out of the main car park keeping the impressive priory ruins, hotel and bar on your right.

Go through the **wooden gate** straight ahead and bear right along the track sign posted for **Hatterrall Hill**.

Pass through another **gate** and continue along the track. See the flanks of Hatterrall Ridge ahead of you.

At the path junction, turn left signed for **All Routes**; this is a detour to avoid walking through private land.

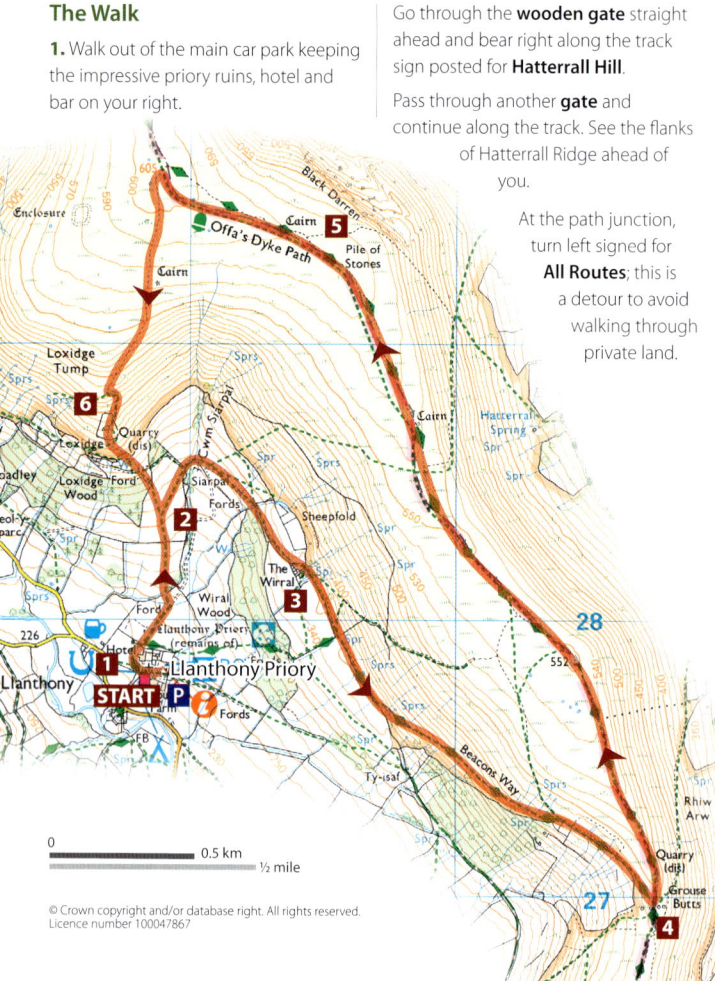

Walk 9 – **Llanthony Priory & Hatterrall Ridge**

Walking back to Llanthony Priory

Pass through the gate, still following signs for Hatterrall Ridge, and up the **field** dotted with skeletons of fallen oak trees.

2. Branch right when you are about half-way through the field. Aim for the **stile and gate** in the north-east corner of the field.

Cross the stile and walk along the track, passing the ruins of **Siarpal** on the right.

Siarpal, or Y Siarpal, is believed to be the ruins of an incomplete mansion house. It was owned by Walter Savage Landor in the early 1800's. He was an English writer and poet who was fond of this area of South Wales.

Continue ahead along the clear track which is now signposted for Wirral.

3. Arrive at **Wirral** — a secluded house at the foot of the tree line — and cross the stile into the wood behind the house, sign posted for **Hatterrall Ridge**.

Continue steadily uphill on this traversing path which is eventually joined by the Beacons Way. The path becomes steeper as it leads you towards the ridge top.

Llanthony Priory and Hatterrall Ridge

Be on the lookout for herds of Welsh mountain ponies. Their sturdy, strong build is ideal for living in exposed and tough climates. These semi-wild ponies are believed to have lived in the Brecon Beacons for over 3,000 years.

4. Bear left at the grouse butts to join the **Offa's Dyke path** along **Hatterrall Ridge**. Stay on this high moorland ridge now for some time.

Pass the trig point marking 552m in elevation and then, a short while later, pass a **pile of stones.**

5. Pass by another large **stone cairn** on your right.

Continue along the ridge until you reach the path junction marked by a small stone cairn.

Bear left here in a south-westerly direction and make your way downhill towards **Llanthony**.

As you descend the ridge, you'll enjoy exceptional views opening up across the Vale of Ewyas (Dyffryn Ewias) and Llanthony Priory.

The River Honddu (Afon Honddu in Welsh) flows through the centre of the Vale of Ewyas below. The river is a popular and sheltered fishing area. It eventually joins the River Monnow on the border with England.

6. Where the path meets the small **stream**, it curves left to snake down into the edge of **Loxidge Wood**.

Cross the **stile** and bear right towards Llanthony Priory. Pass through the clearing. Cross **two more stiles** and then bear right, signed for Llanthony.

Continue following **signs for Llanthony** to return to your starting point. ♦

Offa's Dyke

177 miles / 285 kilometres of waymarked trail make up the Offa's Dyke long distance footpath, which follows the Wales/England border linking Sedbury Cliffs near Chepstow in the south with the seaside town of Prestatyn in the north. The trail passes through eight different counties, both Welsh and English. To complete the trail in one go is quite a challenge, generally taking a fit walker around 12 days.

The Skirrid Inn

PUB WALK

walk 10

The Skirrid Mountain Inn

Walk through countryside to climb The Skirrid before returning to one of the oldest public houses in Wales

What to expect:
Pretty countryside, way-marked paths for the majority, steep ascent and descent

Distance/time: 10.5 kilometres / 6.5 miles. Allow 4 hours
Start: Roadside parking in Llanvihangel Crucorney
Grid ref: SO 326 205
Ordnance Survey Map: OS Explorer OL13 Brecon Beacons National Park *Eastern area*
The Pub: The Skirrid Mountain Inn, Llanvihangel Crucorney NP7 8DH | 01873 890 258

Walk outline

Plenty of variety means this walk should not be missed! Follow the Beacons Way through tracks and beautifully lush countryside. A quiet lane section leads to the base of The Skirrid (Ysgyryd Fawr in Welsh, or also known as Skirrid Fawr) where the route meanders up the mountainside. Gain height surprisingly quickly to reach the summit. Descend the scenic ridge on easy-to-follow paths and into a sheltered forest, where the route curves around the foot of The Skirrid to re-join a quiet lane. Footpaths through fields and across roads lead back to The Skirrid Mountain Inn.

Mountain dog

▶ The Skirrid Inn at a glance

Open: Every day – check times in advance.
Ales and wine: Wye Valley Bitter plus more choice.
Food: Good pub food with generous portion sizes. Vegetarian options.
Outside: Rear beer garden with umbrellas plus seating at the front. Car park and roadside parking.
Children & dogs: Well behaved children and dogs welcome.
Accommodation: Rooms available to book in advance.
Ghost hunts: The inn is considered one of the most haunted in Wales and holds regular ghost hunt events — call 01873 890 258 for details.

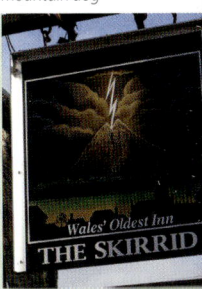

The Walk

1. Park on the roadside outside **The Skirrid Mountain Inn** in the village of Llanvihangel Crucorney. Walk south-west along the road with the inn on your right.

You are on **The Beacons Way**; a long-distance trail through the entire Brecon Beacons National Park.

Opposite **St Michael's Church**, bear left down the walkway.

Take care **crossing the road** and walk down the lane ahead towards **Llanvihangel Court**, an impressive Tudor manor house and estate.

The lane becomes grassier and more overgrown, especially in summer.

Just past the **farm storage buildings**, take the gate on the right waymarked for **The Beacons Way**.

Continue through numerous fields and gates, following the **waymarkers**.

Eventually, pass through the small wood and cross a **wooden bridge**.

The first floor of The Skirrid Mountain

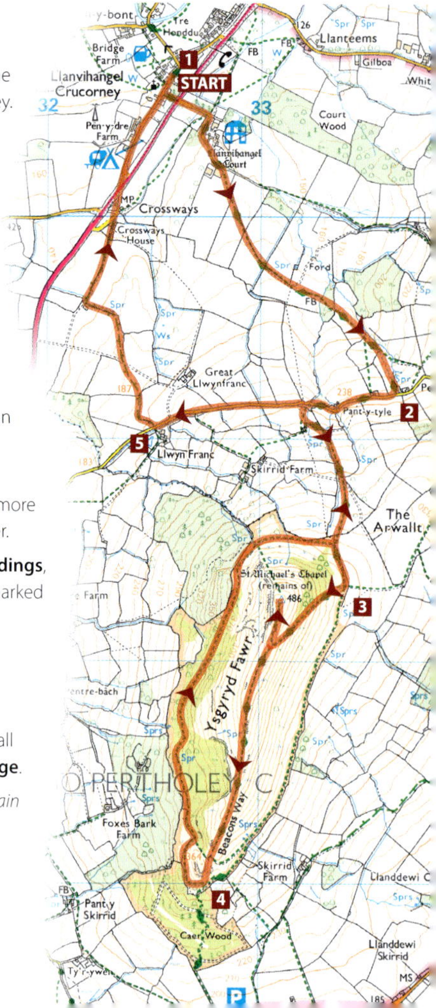

© Crown copyright and/or database right. All rights reserved. Licence number 100047867

The Skirrid summit ridge

Inn was historically used as a courthouse. In the centre staircase you can still see the wooden beam where up to 185 executions took place. It is little surprise that the inn is considered haunted!

2. Emerge from the fields and onto the **country lane** — bear right here and walk along the lane passing several picturesque **houses** and farm buildings.

After approximately 500 meters of walking, turn left over the stile next to a private **driveway**.

Continue gently uphill through fields, still following **The Beacons Way**, below the eastern slope of The Skirrid.

3. Turn right here and walk steeply up the **eastern slopes**. The path zig-zags at first before levelling out.

Reach the main ridge **path** and bear right for approximately 200 meters. Walk in-between two **large stones** to arrive at the summit trig point.

You are treading amongst the remains of St Michael's Chapel. All that is left these days are two large stones. These are likely the remains of an old entranceway.

Summit of The Skirrid

Walk back along the summit ridgeline and continue downhill towards the edge of **Caer Wood**.

4. Reach the **old wall** with a gate. Don't go through the gate, but walk along the **wooden platform** to the right.

This section of the route takes you beneath the western, lesser-trodden wooded slopes of The Skirrid. Occasional breaks in the forest begin to offer stunning views over the valley below.

The path eventually rejoins **The Beacons Way** where you can retrace your earlier steps to the **country lane**. Bear left along the lane.

5. Turn right through the gate opposite **Llwyn Ffranc Farm / The Old Henhouse**. There is a **wooden signpost** for 'Crossways'.

Walk through the field and cross over another **stile**.

Walk in a north-westerly direction across the field, cross a **private road**, and aim towards a **corrugated iron farm store** in the lower corner of the fields.

The path continues from the north-east corner of the farm store.

The route follows the side of a hedge until you arrive at **Crossways**.

Go through the gate, following the footpath through the grounds of the **house** until you join the residential road.

At the **road junction,** bear right and continue ahead.

Cross the next road and carry on ahead into **Llanvihangel Crucorney**.

Arrive back at your starting point and The Skirrid Mountain Inn. ♦

Holy Mountain

Wales is a nation steeped in rich history and folklore. The true Welsh name of The Skirrid is Ysgyryd Fawr, which loosely translates to 'great tremble'. According to local legend, the large fissure in the mountainside happened because of the hill's anger during the crucifixion of Christ. It could also just be the unfortunate result of a powerful earthquake or natural disaster.

Useful Information

Visit Wales
The Visit Wales website offers ideas and activities to help plan your trip to the Brecon Beacons: www.visitwales.com/destinations/mid-wales/brecon-beacons

Brecon Beacons National Park
The official Brecon Beacons National Park website also provides useful information such as local events, places to eat and accommodation: **www.breconbeacons.org**

Tourist Information Centres
Offering free information on accommodation, transport, what's on and walking advice.

> Brecon Beacons National Park Visitor Centre – Libanus, LD3 8ER
> 01874 623 366 | visitor.centre@beacons-npa.gov.uk –
> www.breconbeacons.org/national-park-visitor-centre
>
> Crickhowell Resource & Information Centre (CRiC) – Crickhowell, NP8 1AA
> 01873 811 970 | www.visitcrickhowell.wales/cric-centre

Weather
Online weather forecasts are available from the Met Office at **www.metoffice.gov.uk** or from the Mountain Weather Information Service (MWIS) at **https://www.mwis.org.uk/forecasts/english-and-welsh/brecon-beacons**

Rail Travel
National Rail Enquiries 08457 484950 | www.nationalrail.com.uk

Bus Travel
Traveline Cymru 0871 200 22 33 | www.travelinecymru.info

Camping
The Camping and Caravanning Club – 02476 475 426
www.campingandcaravanningclub.co.uk

Find a list of campsites on the **Brecon Beacons National Park** website –
www.breconbeacons.org/business-category/camping-glamping-and-caravanning